The Copywriter's Workout

A workbook for Wannabe and Newbie Copywriters who want to build strong copywriting muscles

by

Wendy Ann Jones

Copyright © 2023 Wendy Ann Jones

This workbook and its contents are copyright of Wendy Ann Jones. All rights reserved. Any reproduction or redistribution of all or part of its contents in any form is strictly prohibited other than by the prior written consent of the author.

First paperback edition – July 2023
Cover design by Wendy Ann Jones
ISBN 978-1-959555-91-9 (paperback)

Disclaimer: Although the businesses in this book are loosely based on those types of companies that exist in the online space, the companies themselves, their names and the individuals mentioned in the exercises are all entirely fictitious. Any resemblance to real businesses or individuals is unintentional.

www.wendyannjones.com

This book is dedicated to anyone who ever had a dream they decided to follow.

Contents

Introduction		7
What's Inside		11
How to Use The Copywriter's Workout		13
1.	Blue Bahamas	17
2.	Bounce 'n' Party	21
3.	Bubbles Beer Spa	25
4.	Carla's Café	29
5.	Cozy Sleep Direct	33
7.	Diversity Consulting	41
8.	Dressed & Ready Interiors	45
9.	Expert Housing Solutions	49
10.	Flowers 4 You	53
11.	Freedom Accounts	57
12.	Gates Law	61
13.	Hair2Help	65
14.	Helping Hands	69
15.	High-Performance Sports & Adventure Training	73
16.	Medical Marijuana	77
17.	Naughty but Nice	81
18.	Net Zero Advisory	85
19.	Nutronomy	89
20.	Parent Drop-In	93
21.	Planet Food Packaging	97

© Wendy Ann Jones Copywriting 2023

22.	Rosie Flowers - The Finance Coach	101
23.	Shanty's Choice	105
24.	Shelley's Artisan Bakery	109
25.	Stairway to Heaven	113
26.	Sun & Smiles	117
27.	Swiss Holiday Homes	121
28.	The Little Linguist	125
29.	Vignoble Cruises	129
30.	Wasdale Valley Hotel	133
31.	Your Finance Systems	137
Further Practice		141
Acknowledgements		143
Index		145

© Wendy Ann Jones Copywriting 2023

Introduction

One dark morning in February I rolled over to silence the insistent alarm. Feeling groggy I flipped on the bedside lamp. Another day, another dollar as they say — or in my case another quid.

I'd been in my corporate job for over 10 years by that point. I felt uninspired and stagnant. A nagging ball of stress would appear in my gut whenever I thought about being glued to my desk for another dull 9-5 shift.

Avoiding the inevitable I scrolled aimlessly through the socials on my phone.

An ad for a free copywriting course jumped out at me.

"Work from wherever you want, choose your own hours, earn great money"

Was that even possible? I didn't care, I wanted to know more.

I didn't know it then, but that hook was copywriting in its purest form. **It was talking directly to me, and offering me everything I wanted.**

I took the free course. That got me hooked deeper and I started to see a light at the end of the corporate tunnel. *Could I really be my own boss?*

When the paid program was waved in front of me 5 days later — I couldn't wait to sign up. I'd already begun dreaming of my escape.

Soon, I was obsessed with copywriting —

- reading books
- watching YouTube videos
- listening to podcasts

Juggling the 9-5 with my ambition to become a badass copywriter and be a present mom of a teenager getting ready to fly the coop — those first months were crazy. The course was amazing, I felt like **I'd finally found a career that would light me up.**

But I hit stumbling blocks along the way.

Choosing a niche — took months and even then I was overthinking it in every direction. I know of some fledgling copywriters who almost derailed completely at this stage!

Building a portfolio — I didn't have a clue where to start. But I needed to show prospective clients what value I could offer if I was ever going to land any writing gigs.

And let's not even talk about getting a website or making the first tentative approaches to getting clients!

Early on, I stumbled across some work for an online magazine company. It wasn't copywriting. But I spent heaps of time researching and writing about hundreds of different companies in all sorts of sectors.

It opened my eyes to the possibilities — **there must be literally millions of companies that need copywriters!!**

That spurred me on. I began to think I could make copywriting work for me. All I needed to do now was get better!

But here's the conundrum…

How do you get better at copywriting?

Listen to any copywriting guru, coach or mentor and they'll tell you to practise, practise, practise — maybe not until your fingers bleed, but not far off.

But, I had this huge list of stuff I had to do each day (on top of my day job), and **copywriting practice always got pushed to the back** *—*

- ☐ Find clients
- ☐ Do client work
- ☐ Build business processes
- ☐ Network
- ☐ Finish course
- ☐ Listen to podcast
- ☐ Do laundry
- ☐ Buy groceries
- ☐ Pick up daughter
- ☐ Work-out
- ☐ Find clients
- ☐ Cook dinner
- ☐ Spend time with family
- ☐ Practise copy

© Wendy Ann Jones Copywriting 2023

I didn't know HOW to practise,

So I'd put it off until the end of each day — by which time I was exhausted…

And, from talking to heaps of copywriters, I know I'm not the only one.

Surely there had to be an easier way…

What I really wanted was a workbook:

- ✓ Packed with exercises that made it easy to practise my copy
- ✓ Featuring examples of businesses that need copywriters in the real world
- ✓ That allowed me to experiment with writing in different niches
- ✓ And start to build a credible portfolio

There wasn't one — but now there is!

Thank you for buying this book. My wish is that it makes practising your copy easier and more fun and that the practice you do helps you to approach your prospective clients with confidence.

Wendy x

What's Inside

This little book is packed full of copywriting exercises based on real-life scenarios. The businesses in the book are fictitious, but they're based loosely on companies that really exist in the online space.

As well as giving you plenty of opportunities to practise your skills, I'm hoping that *The Copywriter's Workout* will inspire you to know that you're on the right path. *There's plenty of work out there for you when you're ready to take that leap.*

On each page, you'll find a company bio and some basic information I'd get from a client *before* I start working on their copy. It's not perfect, because real life rarely is — it's all part of the workout process.

Below each bio, you'll see suggestions of types of copy you can practise. Use some or all of these, or make up your own – you can always borrow ideas from other pages too.

How to Use The Copywriter's Workout

Everyone has their favourite way of working out — but here are some ideas:

1. Start at the beginning, work your way to the end… and then stop (totally stolen from Alice in Wonderland out of pure admiration)
2. Start at the beginning, but pick and choose the exercises from the options available
3. Dip in at random and pick something that takes your fancy
4. Check out the Index section at the back of the book, and make your choice from there

There are no answer sheets, in fact, **there are no right or wrong answers**. Just plain, old-fashioned examples for you to practise on.

When you've written a piece you'd like to use in your portfolio, consider sending it to a professional copy editor. Their feedback will show you how to elevate your copy to the next level.

If you haven't already, I recommend signing up for a credible copywriting course to get off to a good start. You'll find details of courses, copywriting mentors, and other resources that I personally recommend on my website https://www.wendyannjones.com.

So now it's time to do what you came here to do — PRACTISE!

Have fun!

It's Time to Workout…

Let's Hit the Exercises!

"Make it simple. Make it memorable. Make it inviting to look at. Make it fun to read."— **Leo Burnett**

---

1. Blue Bahamas

Niches

- Travel & Tourism
- Luxury Travel
- Corporate Travel
- Events
- B2B

Background

Blue Bahamas is a luxury destination management specialist. As a knowledgeable local expert, the company helps its clients craft unforgettable experiences.

Deciding on a destination for your corporate event is only the first step. To ensure the event is a success, having a team on board with local knowledge and international expertise is essential. Blue Bahamas has both. With over 40 years of combined experience in the tourism and hospitality industry, the company is well-placed to make sure every one of its visitors has a wonderful time.

Core Offer

Blue Bahamas can help with everything you'll need to make your corporate visit memorable:

- Arrange and plan your meeting, conference, event or gala
- Book accommodation
- Suggest and arrange complementary activities, e.g., golf tournaments, watersports, fishing, beach parties, history tours, sightseeing excursions, cookery classes and shopping trips

Anything you need to make your event a success, we can do.

Target Market

Corporations, large businesses, and sales teams that organise team-building experiences, corporate events or team incentives.

The problem that your product or service solves:

We take the headache out of planning events in the Bahamas. We have all the contacts and expertise to make sure your event runs smoothly. We'll make sure the service is personalised and curated to be one-of-a-kind.

The thing you love most about your business:

Our team. We're multilingual, speaking English, Portuguese, French and Spanish and we are super-passionate about what we do. We want every part of every event we organise to be a huge success for the client.

How you stand out from the competition:

Our local knowledge and our attention to detail. We have wonderful local connections and we never leave anything to chance.

The core message you want your customers to understand:

They are in safe hands with Blue Bahamas, we will take care of everything so that they and their guests can relax and enjoy the event.

The tone or brand image you prefer:

Friendly, approachable, innovative and professional.

What you want the reader to do (the Call to Action):

Contact us to chat about their requirements.

Flex your copywriting muscles:

Brainstorm some pain points the ideal end customer may have

Summarise the client's offer

And, list the benefits to their target audience

Then, choose from:

- ☐ Write an introduction to the Services page for the company website.
- ☐ Write an advertisement to be published in an online corporate magazine.
- ☐ Write a nurturing email sequence for clients that have subscribed to the company's email list ahead of the coming season.

"If it sounds like writing, I rewrite it."— **Elmore Leonard**

---

2. Bounce 'n' Party

Niches

- Small business
- Events
- Entertainment
- Family
- Parenthood

Background

Bounce 'n' Party is a bouncy castle and inflatable hire company. It started out as a hobby for Paul and his wife Sandy in 2019. They would take their bouncy castle to local events and charity fundraisers where everyone loved them. Since then, they've branched out into the private hire sector delivering their bouncy castles all over the East Midlands area (UK). They've recently invested in a second van which means they can take on more orders. This is a small family company that cares about its clients and wants to make sure they have a wonderful time.

Core Offer

Bouncy castle and inflatable slide hire in the East Midlands. Inflatables of all shapes and sizes for any occasion. The company has a giant inflatable slide that measures 21ft long - the largest in the area. Bounce 'n' Party takes care of everything including delivery, setting up and dismantling of the equipment.

Target Market

Parents and grandparents of children under 12. They want their kids and their friends to have an amazing party.

The problem that your product or service solves:

Hiring our inflatables means that the kids are always entertained, and safe. They're a focal point for every party and the kids love them. The parents don't have to worry that the kids are bored or getting up to something they shouldn't.

All our equipment is regularly safety-checked, and we pride ourselves in the way we set it up and explain everything to the customers.

The thing you love most about your business:

Seeing the faces of the kids when they see the inflatable ready to go - they just can't wait to get on there.

How you stand out from the competition:

We're always looking for ways to stand out. We've got bright red vans that kids can spot from miles away. We try to always get the best, most fun inflatables too. But probably the way we most stand out is through our customer service. We've got loads of rave reviews about how we go above and beyond to make sure everything is perfect for our customers.

The core message you want your customers to understand:

We're a family company. We make everything easy, from the booking all the way through to the collection of the kit. We've got packages to suit individual budgets and we'll always do our best to help.

The tone or brand image you prefer:

Friendly, helpful, down-to-earth, fun (we love having a laugh with the customers), and professional.

What you want the reader to do (the Call to Action):

Give us a call or visit our website to book.

Flex your copywriting muscles:

Brainstorm some pain points the ideal end customer may have

Summarise the client's offer

And, list the benefits to their target audience.

Then, choose from:
- ☐ Write a leaflet for the company to hand out at events.
- ☐ Suggest 3 blog topics for the company website. Pick your favourite and write the introduction.
- ☐ Write the Home page for the company website – brainstorm at least 3 possible headlines.

"What I am doing here is taking the reader by the hand and leading him exactly where I want him to go. It seems like a small point and, maybe it is, but it is the little touches like this that keep the letter flowing, the reader moving along, and, it relieves him of the burden of trying to figure out what he is supposed to do when he finishes reading a particular page." — **Gary Halbert**

---

3. Bubbles Beer Spa

Niches

- Wine & Beer
- Travel & Tourism
- Food & Drink
- Health & Wellness

Background

Belgium is one of the beer capitals of the world. Based in Bruges, Bubbles Beer Spa combines two things we love to do on holiday — go to the spa and drink beer. Except this time, you bathe in the beer too!

Beer has a lot of enzymes and vitamins in it that are wonderful for the skin and hair as well as helping to improve circulation and remove toxins. It's a lovely way to relax with your partner or friends.

Core Offer

We welcome groups of either 2, 4 or 6 people for your own private spa experience. There's free beer on tap throughout your visit too which you get to pour yourself. The spa experience lasts for 1.5 hours in total.

Target Market

Tourists and visitors to Bruges who are looking for a uniquely relaxing experience.

The problem that your product or service solves:

It's something different for tourists to experience and it's the perfect way to unwind after a day's sightseeing.

The thing you love most about your business:

It's fun. Everyone loves the idea of taking a bath in their favourite brew!

How you stand out from the competition:

Our spa experiences are completely private, you have your own jacuzzis and you get to pour your own beer too. You'll have over an hour to enjoy the spa and we have a spacious bar to relax in afterwards too.

The core message you want your customers to understand:

This is a novel experience to enjoy with friends or your partner — it's also the perfect gift to offer someone coming to Bruges.

The tone or brand image you prefer:

Fun and upbeat. But not too much, we want clients to know that we take hygiene and professionalism seriously too.

What you want the reader to do (the Call to Action):

Book a session or buy a gift voucher via the website.

Flex your copywriting muscles:

Brainstorm some pain points the ideal end customer may have

Summarise the client's offer

And, list the benefits to their target audience.

Then, choose from:
- ☐ Write a series of 3 short ads promoting the gift vouchers in the run-up to Christmas.
- ☐ Brainstorm 5 possible headlines for the company website and pick the best one.
- ☐ Write an FAQ to advise guests that beer consumption is unlimited during the visit and that they are allowed to bring in other drinks if they want to.

"So, before you begin writing, be sure you know the purpose or mission or objective of every piece of content that you write. What are you trying to achieve? What information, exactly, are you trying to communicate? And why should your audience care?" — **Ann Handley**

---

4. Carla's Café

Niches

- Food & Drink
- Local business
- Small business
- Sustainability
- Events

Background

Since 2009, Carla's Café has served up scrumptious food to locals and tourists alike. Based in Toronto's Queen West neighbourhood, Carla and the team have built a reputation for fabulous food and a warm and friendly welcome. The company only uses locally sourced produce and specialises in vegan, vegetarian and gluten-free choices, as well as its standard menus.

Through lockdown, the café was forced to close, but the team came up with some novel ideas to stay afloat including outdoor catering services for bars and events. Now business is back to normal, Carla wants to continue to grow and explore the events sector.

Core Offer

Outdoor and indoor catering for events and in bars and meeting places where food is not normally served.

Carla and the crew supply all the cooking equipment - including a huge barbecue for outdoor events. With the team at your event, you'll never need to worry about any of your guests not finding something they can eat. Everyone is catered for.

Target Market

Event planners and hospitality venues such as bars with outdoor space, live music events.

The problem that your product or service solves:

We make healthy eating fun. There's something for everyone, and nothing is too much trouble. We thrive in making sure our customers are happy and well-fed.

The thing you love most about your business:

Our team, and our clients. We have the best time at work. We love our locals and our tourists. Taking Carla's out on the road means we get to meet and feed more amazing people.

How you stand out from the competition

We cook the food you want to eat, but it's healthy. It's the food you can feel good about eating, and there's something for everyone. We only buy locally and our business model is 100% sustainable.

The core message you want your customers to understand:

We'll enhance their events with our stunning food and wonderful service. Our food is the real deal, no over-priced disappointing mush. We cater for everyone with our healthy, fun menus.

The tone or brand image you prefer:

Friendly and fun.

What you want the reader to do (the Call to Action):

Call us to make a booking.

Flex your copywriting muscles:

Brainstorm some pain points the ideal end customer may have

Summarise the client's offer

And, list the benefits to their target audience.

Then, choose from:
- ☐ Write a flyer that will be mailed to local businesses to introduce the new service.
- ☐ Write a Services page to add to the Carla's Café website.
- ☐ Write 5 short promos to be used as Facebook or Google ads to promote the service locally.

"Sometimes the best copy to sell a horse is, 'horse for sale'". — **Jay Abraham**

---

5. Cozy Sleep Direct

Niches

- e-Commerce
- Home Decor
- Small business

Background

Cozy Sleep delivers mattresses and beds direct to your door. The company makes its own bedframes and is a reseller of some of the leading mattresses in the country. The difference with Cozy Sleep is that the company makes all its products from recycled or natural materials and the mattresses it resells must meet the same criteria. Jay and Kieron, two friends, started the company after being frustrated with the number of chemicals and plastics being used in the bed industry.

Core Offer

We stock a wide range of eco-friendly, sustainable beds and mattresses. There's something for everyone. Lots of colours and styles to choose from to suit a range of budgets, but without the nasty chemicals. We'll even collect your old bed or mattress and recycle it free of charge.

Target Market

Eco-conscious consumers, young couples setting up a home for the first time, anyone that hasn't changed their mattress for the last 8 years, and older people looking for a more comfortable night's sleep.

The problem that your product or service solves:

If you need a new mattress or bed we can get one to you quickly, often the next day. And we'll take your old one away. You don't have to worry about carrying it or setting it up, we do that too.

The thing you love most about your business:

Seeing how happy our customers are with the service. When we deliver their new bed or mattress you can see them relax. They realise we've got everything under control, and they've got a great new bed.

How you stand out from the competition

Our customer service - we do everything. Changing your bed or mattress can be daunting, we do all the heavy lifting. We guarantee you can sleep on your new bed or mattress straightaway - there are no nasty chemicals filling your house with smells. And our clients know that what they've bought doesn't harm the planet.

The core message you want your customers to understand:

They can trust us mainly. That they're only a phone call or a few clicks away from getting a better night's sleep.

The tone or brand image you prefer:

Trustworthy, helpful, understanding and ethical.

What you want the reader to do (the Call to Action):

Browse our product catalogue.

Flex your copywriting muscles:

Brainstorm some pain points the ideal end customer may have

Summarise the client's offer

And, list the benefits to their target audience.

Then, choose from:
- ☐ Suggest 3 blog topics to demonstrate the client's knowledge of the sector, write one blog.
- ☐ Write a product description for Cozy Sleep's sustainable divan base and headboard - showcase:
    a) the range of colours
    b) recycled and natural materials
    c) delivery and disposal services

"Good advertising is written from one person to another. When it is aimed at millions it rarely moves anyone." — **Fairfax M Cone**

---

6. Discover Music

Niches

- Music
- Music Education
- Education

Background

Based in Asheville, North Carolina, Discover Music helps students discover the wonderful world of music. The company works with students from 4 years old to adults. Its courses include piano, guitar, a full range of band instruments, singing and songwriting.

John started the company in 2010. Since then, he and his experienced team have been guiding and encouraging students to develop their talents.

It's hard work to learn an instrument – it takes a lot of time and effort. Discover Music is method-based so that students know how to practise and approach music at every level. The company slogan is 'it's not what you practice, it's how you practice'.

John says: "We help our students develop real-world skills and our company thrives on its ability to build strong personal relationships."

Core Offer

Personalised music lessons based on the interests of the individual student. Teachers and mentors at Discover Music help students create and stick to a study plan and advise them on how to carve out practice time.

As well as our face-to-face lessons, our students also have access to our online learning library.

Target Market

For this campaign, Discover Music wishes to target the adult market. In particular, focus on adults who have always dreamed of playing an instrument or writing a song but never gotten around to it, or those who have tried in the past and failed.

The problem that your product or service solves:

Most people don't know where to start when learning an instrument. There are YouTube videos, but they don't show you how to practise effectively. And without the right advice and encouragement, most people will give up. We help our students develop a practice that they can sustain indefinitely and show them the path to success. The road isn't always smooth but we are there every step of the way.

The thing you love most about your business:

Seeing the transformation. Some students have been with us since they were small kids, and now they are performing professionally. Seeing adults come in that can't play a note and watching them grow in confidence every week.

How you stand out from the competition

Our personal relationships with our students. We are invested in the success of every person we teach. We want them to love music as much as we do. We hold 6 recitals each year to showcase the progress of our students.

The core message you want your customers to understand:

Music is hard work, but it's also fun and satisfying. We're here to help our students every step of the way and to keep learning fun.

The tone or brand image you prefer:

Welcoming, friendly, passionate, and knowledgeable.

What do you want the reader to do (the Call to Action):

Call us to chat about their goals.

Flex your copywriting muscles:

Brainstorm some pain points the ideal end customer may have

Summarise the client's offer

And, list the benefits to their target audience.

Then, choose from:
- ☐ Write a local flyer promoting Discover Music's services.
- ☐ Write a series of 5 Facebook Ads to promote the 1-2-1 service to adults wanting to start learning an instrument.
- ☐ Brainstorm an opt-in for the company website that will promote this service and write the pop-up asking visitors to download it.

"People will do anything for those who encourage their dreams, justify their failures, allay their fears, confirm their suspicions, and help them throw rocks at their enemies." — **Blair Warren**

---

7. Diversity Consulting

Niches

- Inclusion & Diversity
- Consulting
- B2B

Background

Based in Manchester, UK, Diversity Consulting helps businesses, corporations and organisations along their inclusion and diversity journey.

Evidence suggests that many businesses and public institutions do not reflect the diversity of society. Conscious and unconscious bias, and discrimination still undermine the skills, experience and ideas of many in the workplace. This has a far-reaching impact not only on society, but on the organisations themselves. Diversity Consulting uses learning solutions, mentoring and coaching to help unlock potential and exceed expectations.

Core Offer

Our services help companies and organisations to understand how to attract, develop and retain the right talent. At the end of the day, a happy inclusive workforce is more healthy and more productive. Our clients report better customer satisfaction and better bottom-line results.

We offer staff training and coaching (both face-to-face and online) and mentorship for senior managers and company owners.

Target Market

Large businesses, corporations and public sector organisations.

The problem that your product or service solves:

We take the guesswork out of making your organisation more inclusive. We have a proven system for creating and improving inclusive workplaces, making them better places to work for everyone.

The thing you love most about your business:

We are working to help everyone achieve their full potential. It's fantastic to see the results our clients achieve after working with us, even for a short time.

How you stand out from the competition

We use a blend of our trademarked workshops, coaching and mentoring. Understanding that we all have different abilities that can contribute to our collective future is key. Our CEO, James, worked in the global finance industry for over 20 years, so we understand the diversity challenges faced by businesses and know how to overcome them.

The core message you want your customers to understand:

We're here for you every step of the way. We can help you build trust and transform performance and productivity.

The tone or brand image you prefer:

Knowledgeable, empathic, passionate.

What you want the reader to do (the Call to Action):

Contact us by phone or use the contact form on the website.

Flex your copywriting muscles:

Brainstorm some pain points the ideal end customer may have

Summarise the client's offer

And, list the benefits to their target audience.

Then, choose from:
- ☐ Write an About section that concentrates on the struggles of the client and how Diversity Consulting can help.
- ☐ Write the meta-data for the company's Home page.
- ☐ Identify 3 blog topics and write the intro and CTA for one of them.

"The mind thinks in pictures, you know. One good illustration is worth a thousand words. But one clear picture built up in the reader's mind by your words is worth a thousand drawings, for the reader colors that picture with his own imagination, which is more potent than all the brushes of all the world's artists." — **Robert Collier**

---

8. Dressed & Ready Interiors

Niches

- Interior Design
- Real Estate

Background

Dressed & Ready Interiors is the brainchild of college friends Johnny and Emma. The pair spotted a gap in the market for home staging 10 years ago and Dressed & Ready was born. Working with premium estate agents, the company creates dreamy interiors that help homes appeal to as many potential buyers as possible. This limits the time the property spends on the market and often enables the seller to command a higher price.

Core Offer

Home-staging service. Get your home ready to sell and stand out in the crowded marketplace. Work with the experts to take the guesswork out of what will look good. Don't spend heaps of money trying to work out what buyers want when home staging can achieve better results.

Target Market

We want to attract more estate agents/realtors. This is a quick and easy way to sell our services.

The problem that your product or service solves:

Stops potential buyers from being put off purchasing because of a distracting interior.

The thing you love most about your business:

The results we get. The homeowners are thrilled with how quickly their homes sell. The agents are happy and the buyers get to see the full potential of what they are buying.

How you stand out from the competition

Emma is a published author on the subject of home staging. We were one of the first companies in the UK to be doing this. Our clients love our enthusiasm and belief in the process, and we've never come across a house we couldn't sell.

The core message you want your customers to understand:

Home staging is a great investment for selling your home. It not only makes the home look perfect for potential buyers, it also means you command a higher purchase price.

The tone or brand image you prefer:

Knowledgeable, enthusiastic, positive, and a little bit of fun.

What you want the reader to do (the Call to Action):

To book a call to talk about our services.

Flex your copywriting muscles:

Brainstorm some pain points the ideal end customer may have

Summarise the client's offer

And, list the benefits to their target audience.

Choose from:
- ☐ Write an introductory email and one follow-up that Dressed & Ready can send out to estate agents/realtors to introduce themselves.
- ☐ Think of an opt-in Dressed & Ready can add to their website and write the hook (and if you like, the opt-in too).
- ☐ Come up with a headline, sub-head and some text for the company website to promote its services (above the fold).

"The most important persuasion tool you have in your entire arsenal is integrity." — **Zig Ziglar**

---

9. Expert Housing Solutions

Niches

- Construction
- Sustainability
- Modular Housing
- B2B

Background

Expert Housing Solutions specialises in providing housing to those in immediate need. They've provided housing across the globe to areas hit by earthquakes and other natural disasters. Their homes are also used as homeless shelters in urban areas. The company's eco-friendly modular buildings produce much less waste than traditional construction methods. Expert Housing Solutions is working towards zero energy costs and carbon emissions.

Company CEO, Shelley Peters, says:

"We want to end fuel poverty and homelessness. We don't want people to make a choice of whether to 'heat or eat'. Our buildings guarantee good levels of comfort and meet minimum space requirements. They are built using reinforced steel and are fully recyclable."

Core Offer

Bespoke, modular housing that satisfies building and planning regulations, provides good levels of comfort and is sustainable to run.

Target Market

Social housing providers, local councils.

The problem that your product or service solves:

The need for affordable, sustainable social and emergency housing.

The thing you love most about your business:

Everything! We're on a mission to improve lives.

How you stand out from the competition:

Our modelling capabilities. We can come up with a design and then model it to understand how much energy it will need, the level of thermal comfort, and the acoustics before we start to build. We can justify the design and make the best material choices.

The core message you want your customers to understand:

We don't just sell an off-the-shelf product, we'll work with our customers to get the right design(s) for their needs, quickly.

The tone or brand image you prefer:

Passionate, professional, and reliable.

What you want the reader to do (the Call to Action):

Contact us via email or phone.

Flex your copywriting muscles:

Brainstorm some pain points the ideal end customer may have

Summarise the client's offer

And, list the benefits to their target audience.

Then, choose from:
- ☐ Write the About section for the company website (remember to include a CTA).
- ☐ Research and write a blog about the benefits of modular housing.
- ☐ Write a short magazine ad to feature in a publication aimed at housing trusts.

"On average, five times as many people read the headline as read the body copy. When you have written your headline, you have spent eighty cents out of your dollar." — **David Ogilvy**

---

10. Flowers 4 You

Niches

- Florists
- e-Commerce
- Home Decor
- Luxury

Background

Jayne has been running her florist shop for over 20 years. But when the pandemic hit she knew she needed to take drastic action to keep the business afloat. That was when she took her bricks and mortar business online.

Sourcing the freshest flowers from ethical farms around the world, Flowers 4 You arranges them with all the love and care you'd get from your local florist shop. From a single stem to a stunning bouquet or arrangement, every order is fulfilled precisely.

The company is committed to sustainable practices. All packaging is recyclable and Flowers 4 You is working towards zero landfill. They even show customers how to press their flowers to keep them looking good for longer.

Core Offer

Flowers 4 You recently launched an exclusive subscription service - Especially 4 You. The service offers unlimited free deliveries, complimentary gifts and exclusive access to special offers and events.

Target Market

Anyone that loves to fill their home with flowers and gift flowers on a regular basis. It's anticipated that the market for this service will be people who have a mid to high income.
Possibly small business owners too such as salons, nail bars, and restaurants.

The problem that your product or service solves:

Having flowers in your home or business brightens everything up. They're a lovely focal point for you and your guests. They're also a wonderful way to brighten someone's day - they don't have to be for a special occasion.

The thing you love most about your business:

We love delivering joy to people's doors. We get so many thank you notes, it's wonderful.

How you stand out from the competition:

We're doing everything we can to reduce the ecological impact of our service. We no longer use plastic. We've swapped ribbons for raffia, and our flower food packaging is compostable. We want our clients to enjoy their flowers knowing that they come from a 'green' company.

The core message you want your customers to understand:

We put our heart and soul into every order. We want every client to be delighted with their flowers.

The tone or brand image you prefer:

Caring, welcoming, happy - like a beautiful sunflower!

What you want the reader to do (the Call to Action):

Subscribe to our new service.

Flex your copywriting muscles:

Brainstorm some pain points the ideal end customer may have

Summarise the client's offer

And, list the benefits to their target audience.

Then, choose from:
- ☐ Devise a headline and subhead to promote the new subscription service.
- ☐ Write the final email in a 3-email welcome sequence (from a flower care lead magnet) - CTA to find out about the subscription service.
- ☐ Write the landing page to sign up for the subscription service.

"Metaphors are a great language tool because they explain the unknown in terms of the known." — **Anne Lamott**

---

11. Freedom Accounts

Niches

- Small business
- Accountancy
- Finance

Background

Sally started her accountancy firm with a clear mission. She wanted to help her clients save money so their businesses could prosper. With her team, Sally takes the strain and hassle of dealing with 'the numbers' so her clients can concentrate on running their businesses. The company prides itself on its alternative approach. The team and its clients are like one big family. Freedom Accounts keeps in regular contact with its clients to ensure everything isn't left to the last minute.

Core Offer

Bookkeeping and accountancy services. For us, every customer is unique in terms of what they offer and what they want to achieve. We tailor our services to what genuinely fits each client. Services include:

- Bookkeeping
- Tax returns
- Payroll
- Budgeting
- Management Accounting
- VAT (Sales Tax) returns

Target Market

Small business owners and entrepreneurs that begrudge the hours it takes them to 'do the books' and who dread doing their taxes.

The problem that your product or service solves:

It takes away the pressure of having to understand and complete your accounts on your own.

The thing you love most about your business:

We think fast, react fast and know that anything is achievable. We love finding new ways to help our clients.

How you stand out from the competition:

We're flexible. We tailor our services to fit the client, not our own financial goals. Our team is adaptable and has a great sense of humour and positivity.

The core message you want your customers to understand:

We don't just get in touch with our clients at the end of the year, we're there to help and support them all year round.

The tone or brand image you prefer:

Friendly, stress-free, honest and knowledgeable. We want our clients to feel relaxed and ready to take on the world.

What you want the reader to do (the Call to Action):

We're holding a series of informative webinars at the end of the month, we'd like our readers to sign up for those.

Webinars will feature our top tips for

1. Budgeting
2. Management Accounting
3. VAT

Flex your copywriting muscles:

Brainstorm some pain points the ideal end customer may have

Summarise the client's offer

And, list the benefits to their target audience.

Then, choose from:
- ☐ Write the pop-up wording for the opt-in on the website.
- ☐ Write a landing page to ask for the reader's email address.
- ☐ Write a sequence of 3 emails asking people on the list to sign up for the webinar.

"Quality content means content that is packed with clear utility and is brimming with inspiration and has relentless empathy for the audience." — **Ann Handley**

---

12. Gates Law

Niches

- Technology
- Law
- B2B

Background

Gates Law is a legal firm that works solely with Microsoft Partners. Understanding that in the UK alone there are over 30,000 Microsoft Partner companies, it was obvious that they would need specialist support. The majority of these companies are SMEs, and the CEO of Gates Law, Jenny Gates, is on a mission to provide them with affordable and accessible legal advice, on tap.

Of course, the obvious way to do that was to leverage technology and create its very own LaaS offering (Legal as a Service). The firm is automating as many of its processes as possible to make them 'techie friendly' via its LawBot service which uses machine learning and artificial intelligence.

Core Offer

Much like many technology companies, the firm offers a monthly subscription service. This covers all legal requirements (regardless of the time required) and makes budgeting easy. This is a revolutionary service for what is often described as a stuffy and slow profession.

Target Market

SME Microsoft Partner companies who do not have their own legal team.

The problem that your product or service solves:

We provide affordable legal advice and solutions. Our clients pay a monthly subscription and have the confidence of knowing they have professional legal advice at their fingertips.

The thing you love most about your business:

We are disrupting a very old and established profession by bringing it right up to date. We speak to our customers in a language they understand, not in legalese.

How you stand out from the competition:

We have a unique niche, we understand the technology and we are experts in our field.

The core message you want your customers to understand:

We speak their language and we are in their corner, no matter how much time it takes for them to understand or resolve an issue.

The tone or brand image you prefer:

We're professional but we're also chill. We may not be tech nerds, but we're legal nerds and that's kind of the same. We'd love to come across as a bit quirky but at the same time show that we really know our stuff.

What you want the reader to do (the Call to Action):

Ultimately to sign up for a subscription, but probably hop on a call first to see if we're a good fit.

Flex your copywriting muscles:

Brainstorm some pain points the ideal end customer may have

Summarise the client's offer

And, list the benefits to their target audience.

Then, choose from:
- ☐ The opt-in on the website is a quiz - *'Is it time to get legal support for your business?'* — write a welcome sequence for this opt-in with the final email CTA to book a call.
- ☐ Write a short landing page with the CTA to subscribe to the monthly service.
- ☐ Brainstorm possible headlines and subheads for the company website - choose the best ones. If you have time, write the Home page section that sits above the fold.

"Effective content marketing is about mastering the art of storytelling. Facts tell, but stories sell." — **Bryan Eisenberg**

---

13. Hair2Help

Niches

- Haircare
- Beauty
- e-Commerce
- Non-profit

Background

Lisa worked for over 20 years in the hair and personal care industry. She worked for a major national brand in the US and specialized in 'hair goods'. She took a break from work when her daughter was born and decided she'd like to help other children.

She launched her online store Hair2Help in support of 5 major children's charities and donates half of all the company's profits to them.

Core Offer

This is an e-Commerce store stocking a range of fashionable hair accessories and innovative haircare products. Lisa is going head-to-head with big national brands but her USP of donating 50% of her profits to children's charities is a big selling point.

Products are vegan and cruelty-free. All packaging is recyclable.

Target Market

Parents. Folks who want to buy quality hair accessories and products, but who also want the money they spend to be used for good.

The problem that your product or service solves:

We provide great-looking hair accessories and high-quality products at affordable prices.

The thing you love most about your business:

Our mission to help as many children as possible.

How you stand out from the competition:

We are completely different from the competition. We are smaller and more personal, we give our customers the best service around and that feelgood factor, knowing they are helping children.

The core message you want your customers to understand:

By shopping with us they are supporting a small business that uses its profits for good. We give 50% to children's charities and reinvest the rest into growing the business.

The tone or brand image you prefer:
Friendly, and approachable.

What you want the reader to do (the Call to Action):
Buy our products via our website.

Flex your copywriting muscles:

Brainstorm some pain points the ideal end customer may have

Summarise the client's offer

And, list the benefits to their target audience.

Then, choose from:
- ☐ Try your hand at writing some product descriptions:
    - o A paddle hairbrush that reduces static and frizz.
    - o Professional hairdressing scissors.
    - o A pearl side hair comb for brides.
- ☐ Write the About section for the website.
- ☐ Brainstorm 3 blog subjects, write the intro and CTA for one of them.

"I understand social proof is one of the most powerful levers to convince somebody to enter your funnel or start talking to you online." — **Aaron Orendorff**

---

14. Helping Hands

Niches

- Lifestyle
- Health & Wellness
- Parenthood
- Senior Living

Background

Amanda launched Helping Hands in 2008 after spotting a gap in the market. As someone that loves spending time with her family and getting outdoors, Amanda understands the importance of being able to get help when you need it.

Whenever you think you could do with an extra pair of hands, Helping Hands can help. The company is a one-stop shop for all things help-related. It operates as a franchise model and has 23 successful franchises in the UK. Originally set up to help the elderly, the company now provides services to new mums, working parents and busy professionals too.

The company is fully insured, and all staff are thoroughly vetted and DBS checked.

Core Offer

The company offers a wide range of services including:

- ✓ Cleaning
- ✓ Laundry
- ✓ Shopping
- ✓ Meal preparation
- ✓ Dog walking
- ✓ Gardening
- ✓ Companionship
- ✓ Escorts for appointments

Target Market

1. Seniors who prefer to live in their own homes
2. Children of elderly parents living alone
3. New mums
4. Working parents
5. Busy professionals

The problem that your product or service solves:

Everyone needs a little help from time to time. That's where we come in, we can take the strain out of domestic chores to make sure you don't feel overwhelmed or isolated. And sometimes a friendly smile and a chat are all it takes to lift someone's spirits if they live alone.

The thing you love most about your business:

We work really hard but it's wonderful to see how we support local communities and make a difference in people's daily lives.

How you stand out from the competition:

Our pricing is really straightforward. Clients can choose from one-off help or regular bookings. We want our clients to be in control of their budgets so we've made our services really affordable too.

The core message you want your customers to understand:

We're here for you, there's no need to struggle in silence.

The tone or brand image you prefer:

Caring, understanding, professional, and reliable.

What you want the reader to do (the Call to Action):

Call us or send an enquiry via our website.

Flex your copywriting muscles:

Brainstorm some pain points the ideal end customer may have

Summarise the client's offer

And, list the benefits to their target audience.

Then, choose from:
- ☐ Write the copy for a series of 5 Facebook ads - each targeting one group from the Target Market section.
- ☐ Write a leaflet to be delivered door-to-door promoting Helping Hands services.
- ☐ Work your headline muscles - come up with at least 5 headlines for the company website, choose the best one and write an accompanying sub-head.

"The more your copy sounds like a real conversation, the more engaging it will be."— **David Garfinkel**

---

15. High-Performance Sports & Adventure Training

Niches

- Sports
- Health & Wellness
- Adventure
- Coaching

Background

John Carter trained and served as a Marine in the US forces. Friends and neighbours always sought advice from him on the subject of physical training. So when he returned to civilian life he began offering training and coaching services.

John is a big believer in the power of the mind and the power of nature and the outdoors. Although he does train clients in the studio, he gets them outside whenever he can. He's a huge advocate of fitness for everyone, no matter what your age or background.

If you have a dream fitness or experience goal, John can help you get there.

Core Offer

High-Performance Sports & Adventure Training is the ideal partner for anyone looking to improve their fitness, get outside and achieve their goal. Whether that's to:

- climb a mountain
- ski in a cross-country race
- complete a tough-mudder
- travel to the far reaches of the earth to explore

John will help you train to achieve your best mindset and physical fitness.

Target Market

Anyone that has the ambition to do something that they can't do right now. They know that they can do more, and they want to — they just don't know how.

The problem that your product or service solves:

I help people to feel good about themselves, to seek something new, and to go for it.
I show them the way to get there, safely. To push their bodies and minds, but also how to look after them. We do a lot of Pilates and breathing exercises. They learn to be in tune with themselves.

The thing you love most about your business:

Seeing the transformation. Someone that wants to do the thing, but they are scared and hesitant. They don't know how. When they get there it's magical.

How you stand out from the competition:

I don't see it as a competition. It's all about finding the right person. Someone you click with. We're often in this for the long haul. It's important we get along, we understand and appreciate each other.

The core message you want your customers to understand:

If you want to do it, I will get you there.

The tone or brand image you prefer:

Positive and warm. I'll be there for them through the tough times, and there will be tough times — but we'll get through them together.

What you want the reader to do (the Call to Action):

Call me or book a call via my website.

Flex your copywriting muscles:

Brainstorm some pain points the ideal end customer may have

Summarise the client's offer

And, list the benefits to their target audience.

Then, choose from:
- ☐ John has a beginner's Pilates video as his opt-in. 5 days after sending out the link to the video, John wants to send a series of 5 nurturing emails. Write the first email in the sequence.
- ☐ Write the 5th email in the sequence.
- ☐ Write the landing page that the prospective clients land on to book a call from the 5th email.

"Make your copy straightforward to read, understand and use. Use easy words; those that are used for everyday speech. Use phrases that are not too imprecise and very understandable. Do not be too stuffy; remove pompous words and substitute them with plain words. Minimize complicated gimmicks and constructions. If you can't give the data directly and briefly, you must consider writing the copy again." — **Jay Abraham**

---

16. Medical Marijuana

Niches

- Marijuana / Cannabis
- Health & Wellness
- Non-profit

Background

Cannabis has been shown to have proven benefits in the treatment of chronic conditions. Medical Marijuana is an information service set up to provide help and advice to the medical profession and the general public. A team of experts host free webinars and educational events focusing on the needs of the patient.

Core Offer

Medical Marijuana hosts live events that address different topics including medical benefits, suitability, dosing methodology and routes of administration. Each session is followed by a live Q&A where attendees can get their questions answered by the expert panel.

Replays of the live events are accessible via the organization's YouTube channel.

Target Market

Anyone that is curious about the medical benefits of cannabis or who is already using cannabis as part of their treatment but wants to know more. We're also keen to welcome general practitioners who are keen to grow their knowledge in this area.

The problem that your product or service solves:

We provide the information that patients need to make informed decisions and to feel confident in their choices.

The thing you love most about your business:

Being there for patients and answering their questions. Being a source of reliable information for anyone interested in the subject.

How you stand out from the competition:

We are a non-profit organisation and as such we're not really competing with anyone but ourselves. That said, keeping up with the latest legislation can be challenging, but we're proud to say that our information is pretty much always up to date.

The core message you want your customers to understand:

We're here to help. Most of the conferences and events we've attended were aimed at professionals in the industry, that's why we wanted to deliver something different, specifically aimed at helping patients.

The tone or brand image you prefer:

Helpful, compassionate, and easy-going.

What you want the reader to do (the Call to Action):

Visit our website and sign-up for a free webinar.

Flex your copywriting muscles:

Brainstorm some pain points the ideal end customer may have

Summarise the client's offer

And, list the benefits to their target audience.

Then, choose from:
- ☐ The company has a factsheet as an opt-in - write the wording for the pop-up asking folks to sign up for the opt-in.
- ☐ Write an email to the company's email list promoting the upcoming webinar. Experts will talk about the medical benefits of cannabis for chronic conditions as well as answer questions from the audience.
- ☐ Write an email thanking audience members for attending the webinar. In it, promote the library section of the website as a way of answering other questions.

"Let's get to the heart of the matter. The power, the force, the overwhelming urge to own that makes advertising work, comes from the market itself, and not from the copy. Copy cannot create desire for a product. It can only take the hopes, dreams, fears and desires that already exist in the hearts of millions of people, and focus those already existing desires onto a particular product. This is the copy writer's task: not to create this mass desire – but to channel and direct it." — **Eugene Schwartz**

17. Naughty but Nice

Niches

- e-Commerce
- Sex
- Lingerie
- Fashion

Background

Founded in Cardiff, UK, Naughty but Nice is the brainchild of high school friends Cerys and Faith. During the COVID pandemic, the company came into being when the pair's physical lingerie shop was forced to close.

Going online, the company could stock a much more extensive range of products, and deliver them discreetly directly to people's homes. Much of the Naughty but Nice lingerie and outfit range is designed by Cerys and Faith who also take on bespoke requests.

Core Offer

The Naughty but Nice website stocks a huge range of:

- Sexy lingerie and underwear - male, female and gender-inclusive
- Fetish outfits and shoes
- Adult games
- Sex toys and fun accessories

Target Market

Everyone that likes a bit of naughty but nice fun in their lives.

The problem that your product or service solves:

We give our audience a huge choice of products that we've personally vetted and verified for quality and safety. Our prices are really competitive too.

The thing you love most about your business:

It's fun and it brightens up people's days. We don't take ourselves too seriously. We love having a laugh and our team is amazing at putting customers at their ease. We know people are sometimes shy or embarrassed when it comes to the products we sell. We understand and really do our best to make all our interactions with our customers simple and easy.

How you stand out from the competition:

Our lingerie ranges cater to EVERYONE. We don't want anyone left out no matter what size you are, or what gender you identify as. If you can't find what you want, tell us and we'll find it for you.

The core message you want your customers to understand:

Who doesn't love feeling sexy? We want our customers to feel their sexy best and we'll do everything we can to make that happen.

The tone or brand image you prefer:

A little bit cheeky. Fun. But also we want people to know that we are super professional and really discreet.

What you want the reader to do (the Call to Action):

We want visitors to our website to feel confident to reach out to us for help if they need it.

Flex your copywriting muscles:

Brainstorm some pain points the ideal end customer may have

Summarise the client's offer

And, list the benefits to their target audience.

Then, choose from:
- ☐ Come up with 5 possible headlines for the brand's Home page - remember the inclusive theme. Write the Home page text (above the fold).
- ☐ Write a Special Requests section on the website for customers to contact the customer service team if they can't find what they need.
- ☐ Brainstorm 3 blog topics that build trust - write the introduction and CTA for one of them.

"The ideas presented in your copy should flow in a logical fashion, anticipating your prospect's questions and answering them as if the questions were asked face-to-face." — **Joe Sugarman**

---

18. Net Zero Advisory

Niches

- Non-profit
- Sustainability
- Energy sector
- B2B

Background

Net Zero Advisory was set up to help individuals and businesses make their homes as energy efficient as possible. There are so many options available, but knowing which ones to choose isn't easy. Net Zero Advisory looks at each way of saving energy including new doors and windows, different heating systems, heat pumps, solar panels and insulation. The company advises home and business owners on the best choices for them, what grants are available and how to apply for them. When a client has decided which options to choose, Net Zero Advisory can arrange installation too. Net Zero Advisory verifies every company's accreditations and competency before appointing it to complete an installation on its behalf.

Core Offer

We are a one-stop-shop providing help and impartial advice on all energy-efficiency products for home and business. We give advice on products, help clients apply for grants, and find the best installers for our clients.

Target Market

For this campaign, we want to target homeowners living in houses over 10 years old. People who know they could improve the energy efficiency of their homes but who are worried about choosing the right measures and potentially the costs too. For retired people or those on low incomes, there's lots of help.

The problem that your product or service solves:

Clients often don't know which energy-efficiency products are best for them. There are so many on the market it's difficult to know where to start. Some measures can be expensive, but with the right help, you might get them for free. There are grants available, but you need to know where to look and how to apply - we help with that too.

Also, how do you know that the company you choose as an installer is bona fide? We vet all the installers we work with and make sure they are fully accredited and supply a valid guarantee with the work.

The thing you love most about your business:

Helping people get the best deal and a warmer, cosier home in the bargain.

How you stand out from the competition:

We're a non-profit organisation. Our advice is impartial and we make sure our clients get what's right for them, not the product with the highest price tag.

The core message you want your customers to understand:

We're here for them, on their side. We're the experts in our field and we'll do everything we can to make sure they get warmer more energy-efficient homes at the lowest cost to them.

The tone or brand image you prefer:

Friendly, open, and confident. We want people to know they can just have a chat with us with no obligation whatsoever.

What you want the reader to do (the Call to Action):

Book a phone appointment with us.

Flex your copywriting muscles:

Brainstorm some pain points the ideal end customer may have

Summarise the client's offer

And, list the benefits to their target audience.

Then, choose from:
- ☐ The company is running a 5-ad series on Facebook - write 2 short ads sending the customer to a survey opt-in.
- ☐ Write a 3-email sequence thanking the reader for filling in the survey and inviting them to book a phone appointment.
- ☐ Identify 3 blog topics to demonstrate the company's authority - write one blog.

"Start with empathy. Continue with utility. Improve with analysis. Optimize with love." — **Jonathon Colman**

19. Nutronomy

Niches

- Nutrition
- Weight loss
- Health & Wellness
- Online courses

Background

Over 20 years ago, Philip published his first book. It centred on helping people to manage their weight by getting back to the basics of what our bodies need. According to Philip, most of us have become so disconnected from our original boundaries, we've gained bad habits which are hard to break. In an almost 30-year career as a nutritionist, Philip has helped more than 10,000 clients regain their nutritional balance and their love of eating.

"As children, we are told to finish our plates so that we can have dessert. We find ourselves eating more than we need so that we can get what we want. Then, by the time we reach adulthood, many of us have grown accustomed to overeating. It's become a habit that is hard to break. This often results in poor health or obesity, and we can no longer eat what we'd like to without experiencing feelings of judgement and anxiety."

Nutronomy is Philip's revolutionary program that helps users get back to basics and find their balance without the need for complex decisions.

Core Offer

Nutronomy Free is Nutronomy's self-guided course. It teaches you how to reclaim the joy of eating and learn how to love your body. Nutronomy Free shows you how simple it is to reset your eating habits so that you can be healthy and happy with yourself.

40 videos, tools and resources, and interactive quizzes.

Target Market

Adults that are unhappy with their weight. Specifically, those who have tried to lose weight in the past and failed, or those who are on a perpetual cycle of trying new diets and fads. The target market knows there must be a better way - they just don't know how to find it.

The problem that your product or service solves:

Nutronomy Free is a process that guides you back to yourself and the correct path for your body. No more fad diets, no more guilt about overeating.

The thing you love most about your business:

Seeing clients reconnect with themselves and banish their issues with food and weight for good.

How you stand out from the competition:

We're helping people listen to the wisdom of their bodies. Our bodies already know what we need to stay fit and healthy, we've just forgotten how to listen.

The core message you want your customers to understand:

This is a process for life. It's about getting back in tune with your body's natural instinct. No more cutting out your favourite foods or counting calories. You will never need another diet.

The tone or brand image you prefer:

Trustworthy, honest, empathic, helpful - an authority in my field.

What you want the reader to do (the Call to Action):

Subscribe to the Nutronomy Free course.

Flex your copywriting muscles:

Brainstorm some pain points the ideal end customer may have

Summarise the client's offer

And, list the benefits to their target audience.

Then, choose from:
- ☐ Write the Home page (above the fold).
- ☐ Readers opt-in by downloading a free e-Book - write the welcome email sequence that leads to the landing page for the course.
- ☐ Write the landing page for the 'Nutronomy Free' course (retails at $130).

"Here's the only thing you're selling, no matter what business you're in and what you ship: you're selling your prospects a better version of themselves." — **Joanna Wiebe**

---

20. Parent Drop-In

Niches

- Non-profit
- Parenting
- Early Years

Background

Parent Drop-In is an online community that supports parents and carers from everywhere in the world by providing support and information.

Manned by volunteer childhood professionals, the site is a fun and supportive place to drop into online. There are a wealth of resources available including articles, videos, daily Zoom sessions and even discounts for online stores.

Parent Drop-In is a free service that asks for donations and patronage to help cover running costs.

Core Offer

Support and advice for parents and carers of children of all ages, from babies through to adolescents. Parent Drop-In is a friendly, non-judgemental space for parents and carers to learn, make friends and feel like they are not alone.

Target Market

For this campaign we'll concentrate on parents and carers of babies and small children.

The problem that your product or service solves:

Helps caregivers to feel like they are not isolated. Connects people going through the same struggles. Supports and informs.

The thing you love most about your business:

The sense of community we have built and continue to build. Our daily Zoom calls are really popular and a lovely way to meet with the people that use our other services.

How you stand out from the competition:

Our volunteers are all highly qualified. We have teachers, doctors, mental health professionals, nutritionists and midwives to name a few.

The core message you want your customers to understand:

Parent Drop-In is a safe, non-judgmental space, but it's also a fun place where there's a real community buzz. This isn't only a place where you come to when you have a problem, everyone is welcome, all the time.

The tone or brand image you prefer:

Welcoming, friendly, and upbeat. Although we are professionals, the last thing we want people to feel is intimidated. We're a fun and friendly bunch. But obviously, if there is a problem you need help with, we have everything in place for that too.

What you want the reader to do (the Call to Action):

Visit the website and sign up for our mailing list.

Flex your copywriting muscles:

Brainstorm some pain points the ideal end customer may have

Summarise the client's offer

And, list the benefits to their target audience.

Then, choose from:
- ☐ Write a pop-up that entices the target audience to subscribe to the mailing list.
- ☐ Write the first email in the welcome email sequence.
- ☐ Write an email inviting the reader to attend a nutrition workshop on weaning your baby.

"Copy is a direct conversation with the consumer." —
Shirley Polykoff

---

21. Planet Food Packaging

Niches

- Sustainability
- Catering
- Food & Drink
- e-Commerce
- Events

Background

Planet Food Packaging was founded during the COVID-19 pandemic when product designer, Claire, was furloughed from her day job. The company is on a mission to help create a world without waste. Designing and manufacturing compostable food-grade packaging, Planet Food Packaging supplies the catering industry with a carbon-neutral alternative to plastic.

As well as selling its products to the food and drink sector, Planet Food Packaging also provides smaller quantities of its packaging to the general public for private events and parties.

This feel-good company also provides a composting service for its business customers and donates a percentage of its profits to community and environmental projects.

Core Offer

Planet Food Packaging products include takeaway boxes, food trays, cups for hot and cold beverages, and cutlery, all made from ethically sourced, rapidly renewable materials. These include bioplastic made from plant starch, paper and birchwood.

The products offer a competitively priced alternative to traditional 'fast food' containers.

Planet Food Packaging sells its products via its own website and through Amazon.

Target Market

The client wants to target small food business owners for this campaign.
Food trucks, takeaways, restaurants providing take-away services, etc.

The problem that your product or service solves:

The food industry generates a crazy amount of packaging. Using our products, businesses are no longer contributing to the global issue of plastic waste. We are a cleaner, greener alternative. And our prices are competitive, even more so for businesses opting for a subscription.

The thing you love most about your business:

We're not just talking about the problem, we're doing something about it. Every new client that moves away from using plastic and non-compostable packaging is a huge win for us.

How you stand out from the competition:

As well as our standard designs, we also offer branded packaging. We can create custom designs for one-off events such as festivals or parties. Ordering is quick and easy and our customer service team are always available to help.

The core message you want your customers to understand:

You might think you can't afford to switch to sustainable packaging - but can you really afford not to? We want our customers to know we're here to support them as they transition to a greener alternative.

The tone or brand image you prefer:

Passionate, supportive, knowledgeable and approachable.

What you want the reader to do (the Call to Action):

1. Visit our website and sign up for a sample pack
2. Sign up for a subscription

Flex your copywriting muscles:

Brainstorm some pain points the ideal end customer may have

Summarise the client's offer

And, list the benefits to their target audience.

Choose from:
- ☐ Write a list of what a customer would want to know to place an order for bio cane clamshell burger boxes. Write the product description.
- ☐ Write the pop-up that will entice the customer to sign up for a sample pack.
- ☐ Brainstorm the contents of a 5-email sequence to customers who signed up for the sample pack - the aim of the sequence is that they sign up for a subscription. Write email #5.

"In writing good advertising it is necessary to put a mood into words and to transfer that mood to the reader." —
Helen Woodward

---

22. Rosie Flowers - The Finance Coach

Niches

- Accounting
- Finance
- Coaches
- Online Courses

Background

Rosie qualified as an accountant over 25 years ago. After only 5 years of working in the industry, she set up her own accounting firm. For 20 years she's helped businesses, large and small, get their books in order and their accounts in on time. Over the years, she's taken a more active role in advising businesses on their finances, spending strategies and how to manage cash flow.

During the pandemic, Rosie took her business online and began offering coaching for businesses and business leaders. She's now developed an online course that she's called 'Put Profit First' that will be launching soon.

Core Offer

Putting Profit First is a 12-week self-study course that teaches business owners how to manage their business finances and cash flow effectively.

The course consists of 6 x 2-week course modules, there is a weekly group Q&A call with Rosie and students also get a 1 hour 1-2-1 consultation with her.

Target Market

The course is aimed at self-employed business owners and entrepreneurs that are new to managing finances.

The problem that your product or service solves:

A lot of new business owners feel really out of their depth when it comes to managing finances. Their cash flow can quickly become a disaster area if left unchecked.

My course helps them to prioritise with confidence. It explains financial concepts in a simple way that's easy to understand. There are plenty of exercises for you to practise to make sure you've really got the hang of it.

The thing you love most about your business:

Watching my clients grow in confidence and understanding. In the beginning, many of them haven't got a clue. By the end of the course, they're comfortable talking about financial concepts and using vocabulary that was foreign to them only a few weeks before.

How you stand out from the competition:

My team and I have already helped hundreds of businesses to 'Put Profit First'. By taking this course online we'll be helping thousands more.

The core message you want your customers to understand:

Cash flow and finances shouldn't be an afterthought. Once they've taken the course, prioritising this area of their business will be easy, and they'll know how to make a profit.

The tone or brand image you prefer:

Friendly, reliable and professional. We're experts at what we do, and we want our clients to know they are in the best hands.

What you want the reader to do (the Call to Action):

Find out about the course and sign up for it.

Flex your copywriting muscles:

Brainstorm some pain points the ideal end customer may have

Summarise the client's offer

And, list the benefits to their target audience.

Then, choose from:
- ☐ Write the headline, subhead and introduction for the course sales page.
- ☐ Write a series of 5 Facebook ads for a mini-course opt-in (series of 3 videos).
- ☐ Write a 5-email series for clients who signed up for the mini-course that eventually directs them to the main course sales page.

"There is your audience. There is the language. There are the words that they use." — **Eugene Schwartz**

---

23. Shanty's Choice

Niches

- Animal Nutrition
- Dogs
- Pets
- e-Commerce

Background

When Paul first brought his puppy, Shanty, home he noticed that the little dog was suffering from a serious skin condition. Shanty was always scratching, even making herself bleed trying to get relief from the itching.

As a nutritionist, Paul quickly understood that Shanty's problems could be related to food. He set out to design a food that would help Shanty to heal and keep her skin healthy.

Today the company makes a full range of dog food that is perfect for dogs who experience skin irritation or digestive problems.

The company also supplies vitamins and supplements specifically approved for dogs.

Core Offer

Shanty's Choice produces a range of dog foods that contain no preservatives or cereals that cause irritation. The food itself is made from good-quality dehydrated meat and vegetables and is cold-pressed to preserve important nutrients.

The offer for this campaign is a subscription model. Clients choose how much food they need and the frequency of the deliveries. When they subscribe for 6 months or more they receive a 20% discount on the price of one-off ordering.

Target Market

Dog owners who want the best quality food for their dogs.
Dog owners whose dogs have skin or digestive issues.

The problem that your product or service solves:

Provides optimum nutrition for your pet without preservatives or irritating cereals.

The thing you love most about your business:

That our clients trust us with the thing they love the most - their pet.

How you stand out from the competition:

We manufacture all our dog food in-house so that we can be sure of the perfect formulation every time.

The core message you want your customers to understand:

All our staff are pet owners. All our pets eat Shanty's Choice. We're happy to chat with new customers, everyone here has the knowledge and experience to help.

The tone or brand image you prefer:

Knowledgeable, caring, meticulous.

What you want the reader to do (the Call to Action):

Sign up for the subscription service. We offer a free sample pack that they can try first.

Flex your copywriting muscles:

Brainstorm some pain points the ideal end customer may have

Summarise the client's offer

And, list the benefits to their target audience.

Then, choose from:

- ☐ Come up with 3 headlines for the website Home page.
- ☐ Write a welcome email sequence for readers who signed up for the free sample pack.
- ☐ Write a short landing page for the subscription service (clients will be directed here from the final email in the welcome sequence).

> *"We have become so accustomed to hearing everyone claim that his product is the best in the world, or the cheapest, that we take all such statements with a grain of salt."*— **Robert Collier**

---

24. Shelley's Artisan Bakery

Niches

- Small business
- Food & Drink
- Bakeries/Baked Goods

Background

Shelley always loved baking at home. Her speciality was her sourdough flatbread crackers. When she met Ryan, the pair bonded over baking. And, when they offered their services to a local creamery on a whim, Shelley's Artisan Bakery was born.

Based in Novato, Northern California, the company uses the finest organic ingredients to make its range of flatbreads, hand-shaped bread, focaccia and sourdough rolls. Shelley's bakes all its products in a traditional stone hearth oven.

Shelley's supplies local cafés, restaurants and catering companies and sells directly to the public in its 5 stores.

Core Offer

It's coming up to Christmas and the company has put together a range of seasonal hampers featuring an assortment of holiday treats.

Target Market

Families and folks looking for an authentic gift to send to their family if they can't make it home. They are also perfect for corporate gifting as we approach the holidays.

The problem that your product or service solves:

The selection of sweet and savoury treats is perfect to send to a group of people rather than buying an individual gift for each person.

The thing you love most about your business:

The smiles that our treats bring to people's faces - definitely!

How you stand out from the competition:

All our ingredients are organic and natural. We really care about what goes into our products, the quality and the taste. All our packaging is sustainable and recyclable too.

The core message you want your customers to understand:

We put love into everything we bake.

The tone or brand image you prefer:

Family business, caring, enthusiastic. We care about all our customers and want to make sure that they are more than happy with the goods they buy from us.

What you want the reader to do (the Call to Action):

Order a seasonal hamper.

Flex your copywriting muscles:

Brainstorm some pain points the ideal end customer may have

Summarise the client's offer

And, list the benefits to their target audience.

Then, choose from:
- ☐ Write an About section and add a CTA.
- ☐ The company has an email list of corporate customers - write a promotion sequence for a seasonal hamper range.
- ☐ Write a seasonal blog with the CTA to check out the holiday hamper range.

"You sell on emotion, but you justify a purchase with logic." — **Joe Sugarman**

---

25. Stairway to Heaven

Niches

- Interior Design
- Construction
- Luxury
- Real Estate

Background

Husband and wife team, Gianni and Paula DePalma are the owners of bespoke stair company, Stairway to Heaven. Paula, an expert in architectural interiors, takes care of the design side of the business. Gianni, a master craftsman, has been building and fitting staircases into buildings new and old for over 20 years.

The company works with homeowners, builders and businesses supplying one-of-a-kind stair creations. Stairway to Heaven is also in high demand for stairway refurbishments for stately homes and for UK National Trust properties.

Core Offer

Our staircase design and fitting service. The staircase, if properly considered, can be the stunning centrepiece of a property. We design our stairs for effect but always take into account safety and ease of use.

Target Market

For this campaign, the company wishes to promote its services to construction companies building high-end new properties.

The problem that your product or service solves:

Stairs and staircases are problematic for most builders. It's a specialist area. We can take away the worry that the staircase won't mirror the luxury of the rest of the building. In fact, it will be the opposite — the staircase will be what people will remember.

The thing you love most about your business:

Making our clients' visions a reality. They have an idea, we take that and consider all the technical implications, add some flourishes and voila!

How you stand out from the competition:

We work together like a finely tuned machine. There are no gaps between the design, manufacture and installation. The vision carries through to the delivered staircase.

The core message you want your customers to understand:

The sky's the limit of what we can achieve. We'll work within the budget they give us to make sure there's no better staircase for their money.

The tone or brand image you prefer:

Luxury, high-end, experts in what we do.

What you want the reader to do (the Call to Action):

Get in touch to talk about their project.

Flex your copywriting muscles:

Brainstorm some pain points the ideal end customer may have

Summarise the client's offer

And, list the benefits to their target audience.

Then, choose from:
- ☐ Brainstorm blog topics to grow authority with the target audience - write one blog intro and CTA.
- ☐ Write the About Us section of the company website to appeal to the target market.
- ☐ The company is placing some paid ads - write a short landing page encouraging prospects to book a call.

"Never write an advertisement which you wouldn't want your family to read. You wouldn't tell lies to your own wife. Don't tell them to mine." — **David Ogilvy**

---

26. Sun & Smiles

Niches

- Dentistry
- Health & Wellness
- Health Tourism
- Travel & Tourism

Background

Depending on where you live, dental treatment can be costly or unreliable. Because of this, some patients choose to travel abroad to have more complex procedures undertaken.

Since 2008, Sun & Smiles has been welcoming patients from around the globe into its practice. The company provides a safe and professional service for smile makeovers in an agreeable location close to the beach in beautiful Antalya, Turkey.

The company provides free hotel accommodation as part of its service.

Core Offer

A range of affordable dental treatments including dental implants, veneers, crowns, bleaching and orthodontics.

Target Market

Sun & Smiles would like to grow its visibility and presence in the UK.

Anyone that's unhappy with the way their teeth look and that may be considering dental treatment at home but is worried about the cost.

The problem that your product or service solves:

Having beautiful teeth gives you confidence. You'll no longer be self-conscious about your smile and you'll be beaming all over your face.

The thing you love most about your business:

The transformation in our patients and how happy they are with their new look.

How you stand out from the competition:

We've specialised in smile transformation for over 20 years. All our staff are qualified to the highest level. Our treatments are much more affordable than those offered in the UK.

The core message you want your customers to understand:

We only use the best products and the latest technology. We have hundreds of success stories and every treatment plan is tailor-made.

The tone or brand image you prefer:

Professional and caring.

What you want the reader to do (the Call to Action):

Contact us for more information.

Flex your copywriting muscles:

Brainstorm some pain points the ideal end customer may have

Summarise the client's offer

And, list the benefits to their target audience.

Then, choose from:
- ☐ Research worries that the target audience may have. Write out 4 questions and responses for an FAQ section.
- ☐ Draft a follow-up email sequence for prospects who have had an initial call but have not followed up to book.
- ☐ Think of 3 themes for social media posts and write one of them.

The vast majority of products are sold because of the need for love, the fear of shame, the pride of achievement, the drive for recognition, the yearning to feel important, the urge to look attractive, the lust for power, the longing for romance, the need to feel secure, the terror of facing the unknown, the lifelong hunger for self-esteem and so on. Emotions are the fire of human motivation, the combustible force that secretly drives most decisions to buy. When your marketing harnesses those forces correctly you will generate explosive increases in response." —**Gary Bencivenga**

---

27. Swiss Holiday Homes

Niches

- Real Estate
- Luxury
- Travel & Tourism
- Mountains

Background

Jan Peters moved to the Swiss Alps in his 20s. He fell in love with the place, met a girl and settled down. That was over 30 years ago, and Jan's love of mountain scenery is stronger than ever. Although he enjoys skiing in Switzerland's top resorts such as Davos and Zermatt, Jan prefers the smaller resort of Churwalden.

This quiet, family resort is perfect for worry-free getaways. Close to amenities, but far enough away from the crowds to enjoy the peace and tranquillity of the mountains.

Jan and his wife, Marie, help clients find their perfect holiday home in Churwalden and the surrounding area.

Core Offer

Swiss Holiday Homes brokers sales on anything from a one-bedroom apartment to a dream villa or mountain hideaway. The company provides a consultation service and an all-inclusive package to ensure clients are supported through every stage of their purchase.

Target Market

Private clients and investors who are often from abroad. Staff at the company speak fluent English, German and French.

The problem that your product or service solves:

We know the area very well and understand local methods of construction. We can help buyers through every step of the process, from finding a selection of homes to look at to navigating the paperwork and legal requirements.

The thing you love most about your business:

Seeing our clients get the keys to their new homes and knowing that they have something that's just perfect for them.

How you stand out from the competition:

We understand every aspect of the market and guide our clients through the process with full transparency. It's important that they understand fully what's happening at every stage of the process.

The core message you want your customers to understand:

We take the time to listen and understand. We are their ally. We're very thorough and will do everything to make sure the process is a success.

The tone or brand image you prefer:

Trustworthy, transparent, knowledgeable, and approachable.

What you want the reader to do (the Call to Action):

Contact us to talk about their dream home. By phone or using the contact form on the website.

Flex your copywriting muscles:

Brainstorm some pain points the ideal end customer may have

Summarise the client's offer

And, list the benefits to their target audience.

Then, choose from:
- ☐ Think of an opt-in the company can use to demonstrate authority - write the lead magnet for it.
- ☐ Write a 3-email sequence promoting an open day at the agency.
- ☐ Find a Swiss chalet for sale on the internet - rewrite the product description.

"I have just finished running the hill five times (4 miles), and I did it in 57 minutes and five seconds. Do you see how this type of personal, specific info bonds the reader and writer closer together?"—**Gary Halbert**

---

28. The Little Linguist

Niches

- Language Learning
- Parenthood
- Education
- Early Years

Background

The Little Linguist is an international kindergarten and after-school club. Based in Malaga in Southern Spain, The Little Linguist is an English-speaking kindergarten open to babies and children up to 6 years. The company also provides afterschool clubs for children from 6 to 8 years.

English is taught through play and activities such as crafts, singing and games rather than classroom learning. Children are immersed in this second language at an early age, and this has been shown to provide many benefits.

Core Offer

Kindergarten and after-school learning for babies and children to learn a second language very early in their development.

Target Market

Young, mid, and high-income families who want to give their children a head-start with learning languages.

The problem that your product or service solves:

We provide all the advantages of an expert childcare service with the added bonus that your child will be having fun learning a second language.

The thing you love most about your business:

Seeing how quickly the children adapt to speaking English and how amazed the parents are.

How you stand out from the competition:

Our staff come from the UK, Ireland and further afield. Having native speakers on the staff makes all the difference.

The core message you want your customers to understand:

They will be helping to secure a better future for their children, but their children will only be having fun.

The tone or brand image you prefer:

Friendly, knowledgeable and professional.

What you want the reader to do (the Call to Action):

Fill in the contact form on the website. Make a booking.

Flex your copywriting muscles:

Brainstorm some painpoints the ideal end customer may have

Summarise the client's offer

And, list the benefits to their target audience.

Then, choose from:
- ☐ Write the automated reply to respond to a contact form submission.
- ☐ Brainstorm 3 blog topics and write the introduction and conclusion/CTA for one.
- ☐ Brainstorm at least 5 possible headlines and subheads for the company website.

"People aren't interested in you. They're interested in themselves." —**Dale Carnegie**

---

29. Vignoble Cruises

Niches

- Food & Drink
- Luxury Travel
- Hotels & Hospitality
- Tourism
- Wine & Beer

Background

In 2010, Mike and Andi Johnson travelled to France from the USA for the first time. They fell in love with the country instantly. The people, the scenery, the food and the wine captivated them.

Two years later they were back to stay. They bought a luxury river yacht that needed some repair and had it completely refurbished. Today the yacht, named A Very Vignoble Idea, can be seen cruising around the rivers and canals of Burgundy.

Core Offer

Vignoble Cruises offers private charter cruises for up to 8 people. There's an executive chef and 2 hostesses on board who make sure guests are well looked after. Mike is the yacht captain and tour guide. Andi oversees the hospitality side.

Cruises are tailored to each group and may include visits to:

- Chateaux
- Wine tasting events
- Cultural tours
- Jazz festivals
- Michelin star restaurants
- Cookery courses

Target Market

This is a luxury, high-end offer, aimed at groups of friends and families looking to explore Burgundy in style.

The problem that your product or service solves:

Our guests are taken care of from the moment they step on board. Nothing is too much trouble. They can sit back, relax, take a sip of wine or champagne and watch as the French countryside rolls by.

The thing you love most about your business:

Showing our visitors the very best of France. Seeing their faces the first time they sit in our onboard hot tub under the stunning night sky is priceless.

How you stand out from the competition:

We are totally committed to making sure our guests get what they want from their visit. Whether that's exploring and having high-adrenaline adventures, sitting back and relaxing, or anything in between.

The core message you want your customers to understand:

This is a luxury service and we are there to make sure everyone in their group has a wonderful time.

The tone or brand image you prefer:

Professional, warm and welcoming.

What you want the reader to do (the Call to Action):

Fill in our booking enquiry form.

Flex your copywriting muscles:

Brainstorm some pain points the ideal end customer may have

Summarise the client's offer

And, list the benefits to their target audience.

Then, choose from:
- ☐ Write the introduction for the booking enquiry form.
- ☐ Write 5 short ads promoting some of the highlights of the core offer.
- ☐ Research 3 frequently asked questions for the website and write the responses to them.

"Every product has a unique personality and it is your job to find it." — **Joe Sugarman**

---

30. Wasdale Valley Hotel

Niches

- Travel & Tourism
- Local Business
- Hotels & Hospitality
- Lifestyle
- Outdoors

Background

This family-run hotel is situated in the heart of the Lake District National Park. Built over 300 years ago, the hotel's decor features rustic wood panelling, oak beams and traditional fireplaces. Having been recently refurbished, the hotel can cater for groups of up to 40 people and welcomes corporate clients, holidaymakers, newlyweds and families. The hotel also welcomes dogs.

There's an award-winning steakhouse restaurant on site too. And the hotel is a perfect base from which to explore by car, on foot or by bicycle. Less than a mile away is Wastwater - voted as the best view in the whole of the Lake District.

Core Offer

The hotel is looking to grow its popularity with lovers of the outdoors. With stays starting at one night, you can even get a packed lunch made up to take with you as you head out to discover this beautiful national park. The bedrooms are spacious and stylish. There's a muddy boot room and a safe space to store bicycles and dry outdoor gear.

Target Market

Outdoor lovers in groups, couples, or families. Folks looking for a short break or week away to enjoy the Lake District to the full.

The problem that your product or service solves:

There's no limit or restriction on how long or short your stay is. We can welcome groups of any number from a single traveller to a group of 40. You won't need to worry about cooking or shopping as breakfast and evening meals are served at the hotel. And for lunch, you can dine with us, or take a packed lunch. There's even a selection of cakes for afternoon tea.

The thing you love most about your business:

We care about each and every one of our customers. We love Wasdale Valley and we're proud to show it off to visitors. Nothing makes us happier than a happy customer.

How you stand out from the competition:

Our location is stunning, you can't beat it. And we'll do everything in our power to make sure our customers have a wonderful stay with us.

The core message you want your customers to understand:

Our goal is for them to have a wonderful time and experience the Lake District to the full.

The tone or brand image you prefer:

Friendly, show that we love what we do and where we are, that we're really knowledgeable about the area and extremely helpful.

What you want the reader to do (the Call to Action):

Book a stay with us.

Flex your copywriting muscles:

Brainstorm some pain points the ideal end customer may have

Summarise the client's offer

And, list the benefits to their target audience.

Choose from:
- ☐ Write a series of 5 ads showcasing the hotel and nearby outdoor activities.
- ☐ Write a nurturing email sequence (3 emails or more) reaching out to past clients.
- ☐ Write a short, abandoned cart email sequence for the company website booking system (2 emails).

"I don't know the rules of grammar. If you're trying to persuade people to do something, or buy something, it seems to me you should use their language." **—David Ogilvy**

---

31. Your Finance Systems

Niches

- Finance
- Accounting
- SaaS
- B2B

Background

Your Finance Systems (YFS) is a small software company dedicated to developing financial software. The company has been in business since 2001.

Based in Canada, YFS offers solutions for multi-currency transactions and accounting. Working with resorts, tourist businesses and cruise ships, the company has also designed software incorporating remittance technology that's of interest to financial institutions including banks and credit unions.

Core Offer

YFS develops products and solutions specifically for each customer's needs in line with industry standards and current regulations. The experienced team has access to an extensive code library which it uses to develop and test new solutions and updates.

Target Market

Businesses working in the tourist industry or who need to do business in multiple currencies.
The three core areas of the business are:
1. Point of sale - shops, hotels, B2C businesses, airports, cruise lines.
2. B2B customers - currency wholesalers, money service bureaux and those trading across borders.
3. Financial institutions - banks, credit unions etc.

The problem that your product or service solves:

We provide robust software solutions that give our customers and their customers a better all-around experience. We develop our products based exactly on our clients' needs. There's no 'one size fits all' model.

The thing you love most about your business:

We build lasting relationships with our customers and our customer service is the best. We have regular meetings with our customers to check in, hear about their challenges and take on board their feedback.

How you stand out from the competition:

We definitely provide a more affordable service than our larger competitors. And our service is much more personalised.

The core message you want your customers to understand:

We listen. We take the time to fully understand their business. Once we've done that we'll get started designing their solution. We'll communicate with them throughout the process and make sure we incorporate their feedback into the solution we deliver.

The tone or brand image you prefer:

We are geeks, no getting around that. We're a little bit quirky, but we're certainly not hiding away. We love working hand in hand with our customers. So I guess, quirky but approachable, open and honest.

What you want the reader to do (the Call to Action):

Book a free demo via our website.

Flex your copywriting muscles:

Brainstorm some pain points the ideal end customer may have

Summarise the client's offer

And, list the benefits to their target audience.

Then, choose from:
- ☐ Write a short 5-ad campaign aimed at the various 'point-of-sale' clients.
- ☐ Write a landing page promoting the free demo.
- ☐ Write the thank you email the client will receive when submitting a request for a free demo via the website.

Further Practice

Worked your way through the book and craving more?

Here are some ideas to keep your copywriting muscles in good shape:

1. **Mix & Match** — use the index at the back of the book to find a type of copy to practise — choose a business or niche that interests you and get writing.
2. **Funnel Your Energy** — choose a business from the workbook and practise building a sales funnel.
3. **Spread Your Wings** — find a business online that interests you. Do your research and then try some of the exercises in the book.
4. **Do it Better** — subscribe to the mailing list of a business you're interested in. Check out their email sequences. Can you rewrite them and make improvements? If so, why not let them know — you could find yourself a new client!

Remember, keeping those copywriting muscles in good shape is essential to building the career you dream of.

I'd love to hear how you're getting on. Feel free to drop me an email to copywritersworkbook@gmail.com.

Acknowledgements

Huge thanks to

My partner, Andy for being my second set of eyes and for your unwavering support — even if I drive you crazy sometimes. My daughter, Eden for your designer's eye and your belief that I can do anything I dream of *(it's mutual)*. The copywriting communities of Sarah Turner's Write Your Way to Freedom and Tamsin Henderson's NEON, for being amazingly positive and encouraging from the start.

A special shout out to these amazing copywriters for being my test readers:

Earl Chee, Elizabeth Gordon, Holley Gruenwald, Mark Norman, Emily Rocha, Maggie Schiegel and Elyse Woods — you all gave me that extra push of belief that this book was a worthwhile endeavour, thank you from the bottom of my heart.

"The written word is the strongest source of power in the entire universe." **—Gary Halbert**

© Wendy Ann Jones Copywriting 2023

Index

A

abandoned cart · 136
About section · 44, 52, 68, 112
Accountancy · 57
Accounting · 58, 101, 137
Ads · 28, 32, 40, 72, 88, 104, 116, 132, 136
Adventure · 73
Animal Nutrition · 105

B

B2B · 17, 41, 49, 61, 85, 137
Bakeries/Baked Goods · 109
Beauty · 65
blog · 36
Blog · 24, 44, 52, 68, 84, 88, 112, 116, 128

C

Catering · 29, 97, 109
Coaching · 41, 73, 101
Construction · 49, 113
Consulting · 41
Contact form · 84, 128
Corporate Travel · 17

D

Dentistry · 117
Dogs · 105

E

Early Years · 93, 125
e-Commerce · 33, 53, 65, 81, 97, 105
Education · 37, 125
Email · 20, 48, 56, 60, 64, 80, 92, 96, 112, 136, 140
Energy sector · 85
Entertainment · 21
Events · 17, 21, 29, 97

F

Family · 21
FAQ · 28, 120, 132
Fashion · 81
Finance · 57, 101, 137
Florist · 53
Flyer · 32, 40
Food & Drink · 25, 29, 97, 109, 129

H

Haircare · 65
Headline · 24, 28, 48, 56, 64, 72, 84, 104, 108, 128
Health & Wellness · 25, 69, 73, 77, 89, 117
Health Tourism · 117
Home Decor · 33, 53
Home page · 24, 44, 64, 84, 108
Hotels & Hospitality · 129, 133

I

Inclusion & Diversity · 41
Interior Design · 45, 113

L

Landing page · 56, 60, 64, 76, 92, 108, 116, 140
Language Learning · 125
Law · 61
Lead magnet · 56, 124
Leaflet · 24, 72
Lifestyle · 69, 133
Lingerie · 81
Local business · 29, 133
Luxury · 53, 113, 121
Luxury Travel · 17, 129

M

Magazine Ad · 52
Marijuana / Cannabis · 77
Modular Housing · 49
Mountains · 121
Music · 37
Music Education · 37

N

Non-profit · 65, 77, 85, 93
Nutrition · 89

O

Online courses · 89, 101

P

Opt-in · 40, 48, 60, 80, 124
Outdoors · 133

P

Parenthood · 21, 69, 125
Parenting · 93
Pets · 105
Product descriptions · 68

R

Real Estate · 45, 113, 121

S

SaaS · 137
Senior Living · 69
Services page · 20, 32
Sex · 81
Small business · 21, 29, 33, 57, 109
Social media · 120
Special requests · 84
Sports · 73
Sustainability · 29, 49, 85, 97

T

Technology · 61
Tourism · 129
Travel & Tourism · 17, 25, 117, 121, 133

W

Weight loss · 89
Wine & Beer · 25, 129

Made in United States
Troutdale, OR
05/30/2024